THE POT THAT JUAN BUILT

Lee & Low Books Inc.
New York

THE POT THAT JUAN BUILT

BY NANCY ANDREWS-GOEBEL

PICTURES BY DAVID DIAZ

PHOTOGRAPH CREDITS

Photographs of Mata Ortiz, "Polishing a pot," and last photograph in the Afterword: Nancy Andrews-Goebel.
All other photographs in the Afterword: Michael Wisner. Used with permission.

Manufactured in the United States of America by Worzalla Publishing Company

Book Design by David Diaz
Book Production by The Kids at Our House

The text is set in Jericho and Gustav, created by the illustrator.
The illustrations are rendered in Adobe Photoshop.

(HC) 20 19 18 17 16 15 14
(PB) 20 19 18 17 16 15 14 13 12 11 10 9
First Edition

Library of Congress Cataloging-in-Publication Data
Andrews-Goebel, Nancy.
The pot that Juan built / by Nancy Andrews-Goebel ; illustrated by David Diaz.
p. cm.
Summary: A cumulative rhyme summarizes the life's work of renowned
Mexican potter, Juan Quezada. Additional information describes the
process he uses to create his pots after the style of the Casas Grandes people.
ISBN 978-1-58430-038-0 (HC)   ISBN 978-1-60060-848-3 (PB)
1. Quezada, Juan—Juvenile literature. 2. Pottery—Technique—
Juvenile literature. [1.Quezada, Juan. 2. Potters.] I. Diaz, David, ill. II. Title.
NK4210.Q49 A87 2002   738l.092—dc21   2001038139

FSC
www.fsc.org
MIX
Paper from
responsible sources
FSC® C002589

For a free Teacher's Guide and more information about this book, visit leeandlow.com/books.

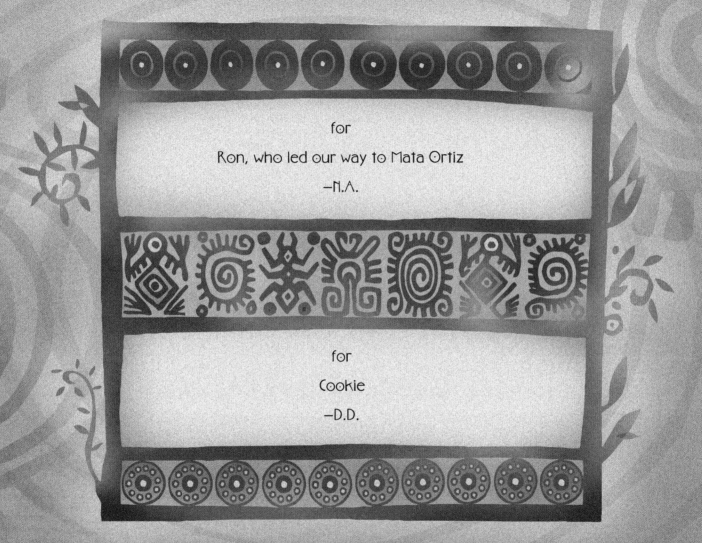

for
Ron, who led our way to Mata Ortiz
—N.A.

for

Cookie

—D.D.

This is the pot that Juan built.

Juan Quezada was born in Santa Barbara Tutuaca, Mexico, in 1940. When he was one year old, his family moved to Mata Ortiz, a village of dirt roads and adobe houses on the windswept plains of Chihuahua. It was there that Juan rediscovered the pottery-making process of the Casas Grandes people, who had vanished from that part of Mexico six hundred years ago.

These are the flames so sizzling hot
That flickered and flared and fired the pot,
The beautiful pot that Juan built.

Juan became a professional potter in the 1970s. Before that he worked as a farm laborer, a railroad hand, a sharecropper, and even a boxer. He has never been afraid of hard work and takes pride in using ancient methods and natural materials in his pottery making. Juan taught eight of his ten brothers and sisters and many of his neighbors how to make pots. They all developed their own special styles. Juan's discovery changed Mata Ortiz from an impoverished village of poorly paid laborers into a prosperous community of working artists.

These are the cows all white and brown

That left manure all over the ground

That fueled the flames so sizzling hot

That flickered and flared and fired the pot,

The beautiful pot that Juan built.

Juan's pottery is fired the traditional way, using dried cow manure for fuel. He gathers manure on the cattle range that surrounds the village of Mata Ortiz. In his experiments Juan learned that manure from cows that eat grass, rather than commercial feed, burns at the best temperature to turn his clay pots into perfectly fired works of art.

This is the brush of hair from his head
That spread the paints all black and red
That colored the pot for all to admire
Before it was baked in the cow manure fire,
The crackling flames so sizzling hot
That flickered and flared and fired the pot,
The beautiful pot that Juan built.

Juan makes paint out of local minerals such as black manganese and red iron oxide. He makes paintbrushes from human hair. He says that some of his best brushes are fashioned from children's hair, especially his granddaughter's. Since very little hair is used to make a paintbrush, no one minds giving Juan just a snip to design a pot.

These are the rocks of red and black
Brought down from the mountain on burro-back
To make into paint all black and red
Spread with the brush of hair from his head
That colored the pot for all to admire
Before it was baked in the cow manure fire,
The crackling flames so sizzling hot
That flickered and flared and fired the pot,
The beautiful pot that Juan built.

When he was twelve years old, while bringing firewood down from the hills on his burro, Juan found his first potsherds. They were pieces of broken pottery from the ancient Casas Grandes city of Paquimé, which was located fifteen miles from present-day Mata Ortiz. The potsherds inspired Juan to create something similar. Even though he had never seen a potter at work, Juan began experimenting with local materials. His mother declared that he was always covered in dirt of many colors from his experiments with minerals and clay.

This is the tool that's made out of bone

That rubbed the pot until it shone

And glittered and glowed and glistened and glimmered

And gleamed and beamed and sparkled and shimmered

To show off the paints all black and red

Spread with the brush of hair from his head

That colored the pot for all to admire

Before it was baked in the cow manure fire,

The crackling flames so sizzling hot

That flickered and flared and fired the pot,

The beautiful pot that Juan built.

After his clay pots dry Juan polishes them before he applies the paint. To polish his pots, Juan uses animal bones, smooth stones, and even dried beans. Animal bones are abundant because of the deer hunting and cattle ranching that help feed the people of Mata Ortiz. Smooth stones are available in the Palanganas River, which runs along the eastern boundary of town. Of course dried beans can be found in any kitchen in the village.

Here's the tortilla—slap, SLAP! pat, PAT!
And the sausage of clay so slick and fat
That became the pot, imagine that,
In the wink of an eye and the blink of a cat
Before it was rubbed with a piece of bone
Over and over until it shone
To show off the paints all black and red
Spread with the brush of hair from his head
That colored the pot for all to admire
Before it was baked in the cow manure fire,
The crackling flames so sizzling hot
That flickered and flared and fired the pot,
The beautiful pot that Juan built.

Juan hand builds all his pots. He begins by patting out a flat piece of clay he calls a "tortilla," which becomes the bottom of the pot. He then rolls out a sausage-shaped piece of clay called a "chorizo" and presses it onto the edge of the tortilla, pinching and pulling it up to become the walls of the pot. Juan makes his pots in a small workroom behind his house, often in the company of chickens and his calico cat.

This is the clay all squishy and white
Dug in the hills from morning till night
To make the tortilla—slap, SLAP! pat, PAT!
And the sausage of clay so slick and fat
That became the pot, imagine that,
In the wink of an eye and the blink of a cat
Before it was rubbed with a piece of bone
Over and over until it shone
To show off the paints all black and red
Spread with the brush of hair from his head
That colored the pot for all to admire
Before it was baked in the cow manure fire,
The crackling flames so sizzling hot
That flickered and flared and fired the pot,
The beautiful pot that Juan built.

Juan says his painted designs look best on *barro blanco*, a pure white clay he digs in the Sierra Madre Mountains above Mata Ortiz. He uses the ancient designs of Casas Grandes potters for inspiration, but he doesn't copy them. Juan never plans the decoration in advance. He lets the pattern develop as he paints it onto the clay pot.

These are the ants that led the way

And showed Juan a vein of special clay,

The very best clay all squishy and white

Dug in the hills from morning till night

To make the tortilla—slap, SLAP! pat, PAT!

And the sausage of clay so slick and fat

That became the pot, imagine that,

In the wink of an eye and the blink of a cat

Before it was rubbed with a piece of bone

Over and over until it shone

To show off the paints all black and red

Spread with the brush of hair from his head

That colored the pot for all to admire

Before it was baked in the cow manure fire,

The crackling flames so sizzling hot

That flickered and flared and fired the pot,

The beautiful pot that Juan built.

One day while Juan was out searching for minerals and clay, he noticed a colony of ants burdened with tiny cargoes of white material. Looking closely, Juan realized that the ants were transporting bits of clay from underground up to the edge of their anthill. So Juan dug a hole near the anthill and unearthed a vein of white clay, the finest clay he had ever seen.

This is the cock that crowed at dawn

That greeted the village and woke up Juan

To ride the range at break of day

Gathering rocks and hunting for clay,

The very best clay all squishy and white

Dug in the hills from morning till night

To make the tortilla—slap, SLAP! pat, PAT!

And the sausage of clay so slick and fat

That became the pot, imagine that,

In the wink of an eye and the blink of a cat

Before it was rubbed with a piece of bone

Over and over until it shone

To show off the paints all black and red

Spread with the brush of hair from his head

That colored the pot for all to admire

Before it was baked in the cow manure fire,

The crackling flames so sizzling hot

That flickered and flared and fired the pot,

Juan gave away his first pots as gifts to family and friends. Today his work is exhibited in museums and art galleries all over the world. In 1999, Mexico's president, Ernesto Zedillo, presented Juan with the National Arts and Science Award, the highest honor for any artist in Mexico. Pope John Paul II received a Juan Quezada pot as a gift from the people of Mexico. In spite of his fame and wealth, Juan cherishes most of all the time he spends in solitude, exploring the hills above Mata Ortiz in search of minerals and clay. If he is very quiet, Juan says, the voices of the ancient potters can still be heard.

The beautiful pot that Juan built.

AFTERWORD

Juan Quezada's story is closely connected to his people and his land. His village, Mata Ortiz, lies on the high windswept grasslands of northern Chihuahua, between the Palanganas River and the foothills of the Sierra Madre Mountains in northern Mexico. The history of Mata Ortiz and its surroundings is richly diverse. The area was home to the Casas Grandes civilization from the eleventh through the fourteenth centuries. Later, Apache tribal people occupied the region for about three hundred years. At the end of the nineteenth century Mexican troops forced the Apache tribes to leave that part of Mexico. Mormon farmers from the United States then immigrated into the area, and Chinese immigrants and other new arrivals began settling in Mata Ortiz to work on the railroad.

MATA ORTIZ TODAY

During the Mexican Revolution of 1910 to 1917, soldiers from opposing sides battled throughout the region, causing many people to flee. After the revolution, Mata Ortiz was home mainly to railroad workers and others who found jobs as seasonal laborers in nearby Mormon orchards and packing houses. Local farm labor income was supplemented by fieldwork in the United States and whatever cattle ranching and farming families could manage on their own at home. Until the 1980s life was very hard and family incomes were barely enough to feed, clothe, and educate the children of Mata Ortiz.

Today Mata Ortiz looks much the same as it did back in the early 1980s. Burros still wander along dusty lanes

lined with modest adobe houses and the occasional shade tree. Sandal-shod children play in the streets with the simplest of toys, while women, forever battling dust with brooms and buckets of water, keep watch over them. Old men returning on foot from the nearby fields, tools resting on their shoulders, give no hint of the amazing transformation that has occurred in Mata Ortiz.

In 1976 an anthropologist named Spencer MacCallum came accross some remarkable pots in a second-hand shop in southern New Mexico. MacCallum became so interested in the pieces that he set off for the Mexican *frontera* and found the pots' creator, Juan Quezada, in Mata Ortiz. Juan explained to the visiting anthropologist that he hand built the pots, using only local natural materials. He told MacCallum that ever since finding ancient potsherds as a child, he had known he could create

JUAN QUEZADA
WITH ONE OF HIS POTS

pottery from the natural resources around Mata Ortiz. After twenty years of experiments he had succeeded in recreating the primitive pot-making process of the Casas Grandes people. Spencer MacCallum encouraged the talented young artist to continue his work while he introduced Juan's pottery to art patrons in the United States. Motivated by growing interest and recognition, Juan began producing more and better pots. He taught his family and neighbors to do the same and helped transform Mata Ortiz from a poor neglected village into a community of world-famous artists.

Now more than four hundred artists live and work in Mata Ortiz, a village with a population of only two thousand. Nearly every house is home to at least one potter, and some households are completely made up of artists. Styles vary from potter to potter, but the same pot-making process is shared by nearly all.

Juan digs clay with a pick and shovel in the rugged foothills outside the village. When he returns home with a load of clay, he cleans the material by soaking it in buckets of water for several days.

DIGGING FOR CLAY

CLEANING THE CLAY

When the clay is slushy enough to pour, he runs it through a strainer made of old fabric. The fine liquid clay that passes through the strainer is left to settle until it becomes solid enough to work.

Juan wedges the cleaned clay, kneading out any air pockets. The wedged clay is then patted into a "tortilla" that in turn is placed in a *puki*, a shallow bowl used for support. Another lump of clay is rolled into a sausage shape called a

ADDING THE CHORIZO

"chorizo." Juan then wraps the chorizo around the edge of the tortilla and meticulously pinches and pulls up the walls of the pot to give shape to the new pot, or

SHAPING A POT

olla. The pot is then left to dry for a few days until it is ready to be sanded and polished.

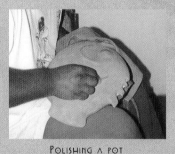
POLISHING A POT

When the pot is dry, Juan removes it from the puki, rubs the surface with sandpaper (one of the few modern materials allowed), and then polishes the pot with a small stone, deer bone, or bean. The polishing takes hours, sometimes days, and gives the pot a nearly mirrored surface that serves as a "canvas" for the painted design.

GRINDING MINERALS
FOR PAINT

The fluid dance of paint against clay, so characteristic of Juan's pottery, is achieved with a long slender brush made of a few strands of human hair. The paint is made from minerals that are found, among other places, in abandoned mines in the hills above the village. Juan grinds the minerals into powder using a *metate*, a traditional grinding stone. Then he mixes the mineral powder with clay and water to create a milky fluid paint. The paint is slowly and carefully applied to the pots in designs that are often based on those of the ancient Casas Grandes potters.

PAINTING A POT

After completing the complicated patterns of curves and grids, Juan fires his pots in cow manure or cottonwood bark. This natural fuel is stacked around a *quemador*, an inverted clay tub that covers the pot. After the fire is lit, the fuel burns for about twenty minutes. Then the coals

STACKING FUEL
AROUND A QUEMADOR

are knocked away, and after thirty minutes of cooling, the quemador is removed. Another half hour passes before the finished pot is cool enough to touch. At

A POT COOLING

this point Juan sometimes places a warm pot into the hands of its new owner, a lucky collector who witnessed the entire firing and cooling process.

Museums, galleries, and art lovers around the world prize the beautiful pottery from Mata Ortiz. Nearly every day visiting collectors can be found in the village,

making their way from house to house, hoping to return home with a treasured piece. The people of Mata Ortiz now enjoy the security a stable local economy provides. The simple

ONE OF JUAN'S UNIQUE POTS

adobes have modern kitchens, heating units for the freezing winters, and bathrooms with hot and cold running water. Shiny pickup trucks are found in many backyard corrals alongside the chickens and pigs.

JUAN QUEZADA

Reflecting on the changes the art movement has brought to Mata Ortiz, Juan Quezada observes with characteristic enthusiasm, "People in the village are happy. They no longer have to leave their hometown to find jobs. Their work is here with

their families." He further adds, "The pottery is so important! To me, all the world's pottery is wonderful, but especially when it is produced naturally, in the traditional manner, the way we do it here in Mata Ortiz. I really do believe that it's what makes our pottery so interesting. We'll pass this

JUAN TEACHING HIS GRANDSON TO MAKE POTS

work on to our children and our grandchildren for

ANOTHER ONE OF JUAN'S BEAUTIFUL POTS

their futures, for the future of Mata Ortiz. My hope is that one day the village will have a nice art history museum here in the old train station. It will have big shade trees all around, a pleasant place for people to sit quietly and reflect on their lives and on the past, the present, and the future of our village."